KT-433-842

WHO NEEDS A BOAT?

THE STORY OF MOSES

By Marilyn Lashbrook

Illustrated by Stephanie McFetridge Britt

**CANDLE
BOOKS**

The story of Moses crossing the Red Sea has a continuing fascination for children and adults. "Who Needs A Boat?" will bring the story to life for your little ones and give them a vivid reminder of God's power and protection. After you have read the story to your child several times, allow him or her to fill in the italicised words. The poem on the last page is a paraphrase of the song Moses sang. Your little one can memorize it easily and will delight in saying it with you as you read it.

Copyright © Rainbow Studies International

First published in the UK in 1992 by Candle Books (a publishing imprint of Lion Hudson plc). This printing 2004

Distributed by Marston Book Services Ltd, PO Box 269, Abingdon, Oxon OX14 4YN

Co-edition arranged by Lion Hudson plc, Oxford

All enquiries to Lion Hudson plc, Mayfield House, 256 Banbury Road, Oxford OX2 7DH

Tel: +44 (0) 1865 302750
Fax: +44 (0) 1865 302757
Email: coed@lionhudson.com
www.lionhudson.com

Printed in Hong Kong

ISBN 0 9489 0259 0

WHO NEEDS A BOAT?

THE STORY OF MOSES

By Marilyn Lashbrook

Illustrated by Stephanie McFetridge Britt

Taken from Exodus 3-15

FOR Moses, it seemed like
it was going to be
just an ordinary day.

But suddenly a bush caught fire!

And God spoke to Moses.

"I have heard my people crying," God said, "and I am sending *you* to lead them out of Egypt."

So Moses went to see the king.

"God says to let His people go!"
Moses told him.

But the king replied,
"I do not know God,
and I will *NOT*
let the people go!"

So God sent
frogs to ... *jump in the king's bed*
and flies to ... *buzz in his ears*
and gnats to ... *crawl on his nose*
and grasshoppers to ... *eat his plants*
and a lot of other things
to make the king ... *change his mind.*

And it worked.

"Go!" shouted the king.
"Take the people! Take the sheep!
Just take them all and *GO!*"

So the people followed Moses
out of Egypt. They walked and walked
'til they came to the sea.

There was no bridge.
They had no boats.
How would they get across?

Then the people heard
a noise like thunder,
but it was not a rainstorm.

It was worse than that!

It was the king's army
thundering toward the sea!

The soldiers were coming
to take God's people back to Egypt.

The people cried out in fear.

Moses tried to calm them.
"Do not *be afraid*," he said,
"God will fight for you."

Then God told Moses
to hold his rod
out over the water.

And Moses did.

And the sea opened
right down the middle.

It opened wider and wider.

Walls of water rose higher and higher.

Moses and the people walked
through the sea
on the road God made for them.

What a funny sight it was!

When they were safe on the other side,
the people turned around to watch.

The army was still coming!

Moses lifted his rod,
and *God* brought all the water
splashing down.

The king's army was swished away
never to bother
God's people again.

Moses and the people
were thankful for God's help,
so they sang this happy song:

"The Lord is my strength,
The Lord is my song,
I'll praise my God,
All the day long."

ME TOO!®
B O O K S